CW01635457

from b(... ɯnent

to reality ∽ nothingness to now ∽ invisible currents

flow ∽ open outward ∽ above and around and through

∽ free of thought ∽ reflecting ∽ something within ∽

without ∽ and beyond ∽ words

Figment Books

Other titles in this series:

In a Grain of Sand

Magpie Mind

Available through www.figmentpublishing.co.uk

Figment Books

An Imprint of Figment Creative Expression Ltd.

Figment Books
4 Borrows Gate
Stirling, FK9 5GQ
www.figmentpublishing.co.uk

Printed in the UK.

ISBN 978-1-912099-00-9

A CIP record for this book is available from the British Library.

Contents

Personal Note

Hello, I'm Laura and I'm a procrastinator.

Specifically, I'm a writer who procrastinates about writing. This puts me in a fantastic position to support other writers. I help them to identify their own procrastination demons and defeat them. Wellspring writing is a key tool for this, developed during Figment writing workshops.

This book was initially intended as a blog post, intended to help me take stock and reflect on the free-writing process. As it turned out, there were far too many important things to include for one blog post. Compiling a book also gave other writers the chance to showcase some of their wonderful breakthroughs – breakthroughs I've loved witnessing, as both their tutor and their peer.

Wellspring writing, free-flow writing, free-fall or spontaneous writing (a rose by any other name) is all about breaking loose from whatever inhibits our writing. It's not about producing an end product or about writing Literature with a capital "L". It's a beginning. So extra thanks go to those brave souls who have generously contributed their examples of wellspring writing. These short pieces are not reflective of their overall writing ability (which includes, of course, the painstaking editing process).

The publication of *Wellspring* marks Figment's six-year anniversary – and with it the beginning of a very personal journey. Starting the Figment workshops was a wellspring moment for me – a point at which infinite exciting possibilities opened up. That wellspring still flows today.

I'm incredibly grateful to have become a part of the intriguing hidden circle of society called "writers". It has been a great pleasure to meet and learn from others in this community. I hope that this book can go some way towards supporting other writers, whether they are just starting out or resuming their own writing journeys.

Thank you for reading,

Laura

How to Use This Book

Prompts

I've designed *Wellspring* to work on two levels: both as a writing guide and as a source of quick inspiration. So either way, you've no excuse for not writing!

The prompts at the bottom of each page can be used for your own wellspring tapping and are designed to illustrate how easy it is to find inspiration around you in each and every moment. Some prompts are single words, some give suggestions about places to find inspiration. Use them all in the same way: as a place to start writing as soon and as freely as possible.

About the Characters

Wellspring is intended as a writing support, not a psychological basis of treatment. A little understanding of basic psychology is useful, however, to help writers work around blocks to their inspiration.

For the purposes of this book I've therefore anthropomorphised certain functions of the brain into characters – Muse, Critic, Heckler and so on. These are not intended to imply a schizoid break in personality, but merely to simplify our current understanding of complex brain functions into a more succinct and manoeuvrable vocabulary, whilst avoiding oversimplified notions of left and right brain functions. Their representation as characters is also derived from the therapeutic approach of Voice Dialogue, in which therapists address specific parts of a person's psyche by engaging those parts in dialogue.

Showcase

This chapter contains tips and examples of wellspring writing from writers of varied backgrounds and experiences, all of whom I admire greatly. Thank you again – you've expressed how useful you find the wellspring writing process much more effectively than I ever could. This is perhaps the most important part of the book. Much can be learned from these writers' enthusiasm, generosity and fearlessness.

Toolkit

There are nearly as many books about writing as there are published authors – we all have something to say about this mysterious and beguiling process. I've curated a few quotes from writers much more eloquent than myself that I hope will inspire and encourage. I've also included a list in the appendix of books, websites, apps and other assorted tools I regularly find incredibly useful. Most I reference briefly within *Wellspring*, but they're well worth reading in full.

How to Read

This guide is set up in a rough order. I'd advise reading it in that order, but you may feel some chapters are more relevant to you than others at different stages in your writing journey. So of course, feel free to dip in and out.

First, however, I recommend reading 'Seducing your Muse' and 'Tapping the Source'. These chapters describe the central wellspring process and how to approach it, and so inform every other chapter.

With love and with immense gratitude to every writer that's joined me on my own Figment journey, and all those still to come.

Seducing Your Muse

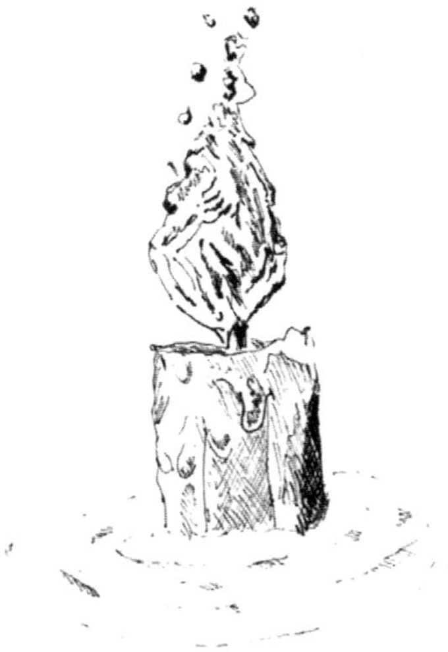

Sometimes, a little preparation can help inspiration flow, so here's some advice to help you set the scene before you get started.

A Muse is a flighty little thing, insubstantial and delicate. It spooks very easily. Communicating with your Muse can be tricky as catching a butterfly in a gossamer silk net. As Ray Bradbury said in *Zen in the Art of Writing*, it will "fly if held too lightly," or "die if held too tightly."

You can't beat your Muse into submission with schedules and plans and structures – those are logical processes better suited to your Editor. Your Muse wants to be seduced. She wants to help you, but you have to meet her half way. Trust is a two-way street, after all, in any relationship. Inspiration will flow from her to you but you need to open up to her first.

Notice your Muse and appreciate her when she appears. She takes offence easily, so respect her. Be on time. Turn up every day when you promised her you would. Don't walk away midway through a conversation to tidy your desk or cut the grass or anything else your Heckler might suggest is a more practical use of your time.

1

Look up – what's the first thing your eye rests on?

I suggest that you also do whatever you can to make your approach to writing a pleasure. Make your writing environment a welcoming space. Use things you love, whether that be vellum paper, a fountain pen, a typewriter or a smart little laptop.

Make a Date with Your Muse

It's useful to set up a regular routine with your writing. This varies for every writer.

Toni Morrison begins before dawn and writes for a few hours. Isaac Asimov started at 7:30 a.m. Flaubert wrote during the night and got up late in the day. Experiment with different times and see what works for you.

Sometimes wellspring writing is more successful when your Editor is a bit bleary-eyed, so try first thing in the morning or last thing at night. I tend to work better in the morning. If I write at night, I get jazzed up with inspiration and can't switch off when it's time to go to sleep.

Making time for yourself is a necessity rather than an indulgence, but that's not to say it can't be a pleasure. Put on some music, maybe light

your favourite colour

some candles. But don't procrastinate! If your ritual is longer than the amount of time you have left to write, your balance is out of whack.

A secret that some writing groups and tutors might not let you in on: to write well, you don't have to take the initial process too seriously. Suffering for your art is not a prerequisite for greatness.

If you want to be serious, if that's your thing, then of course go ahead. There's great depth and poignancy to be captured on the page when you're in a serious frame of mind. There's great enjoyment to be had in that, too.

My point is: if you're not enjoying it, especially in those initial stages, then you're not going to have the motivation to maintain your regular practice, never mind the editing process.

When you're finding it tough to rouse yourself to write, remember what you love about that moment when ideas flow freely:

- old memories resurface – memories you didn't even realise you had
- you make connections between things you'd never before thought could be linked
- problems are solved
- you find focus
- you get to feel inspired, creative and intelligent
- it buoys you up for the rest of the day
- new people are created from nowhere (fictional, but, hey, while you read, they're real, right?)
- ideas hit you from nowhere
- you get to sit back and let things happen – you don't have to be in charge or control anything
- you get to observe as something wonderful happens

Some additional tips, including those from writers I know:

- Read a poem before you write. There are some brilliant collections out there. One of my favourites is *Rattle Bag*, edited by Seamus Heaney and Ted Hughes.

- You could also sign up on any of several websites to receive a daily poem via e-mail (for example, The Poetry Foundation).

- Listen to music. Vary what you listen to, perhaps depending on the mood of the scene you are writing. Lots of writers find songs distracting – all those words can intrude and influence your writing. So you may prefer to use some instrumental music, whether it be classical or synth.

an imaginary place you would meet your Muse

Tapping the Source

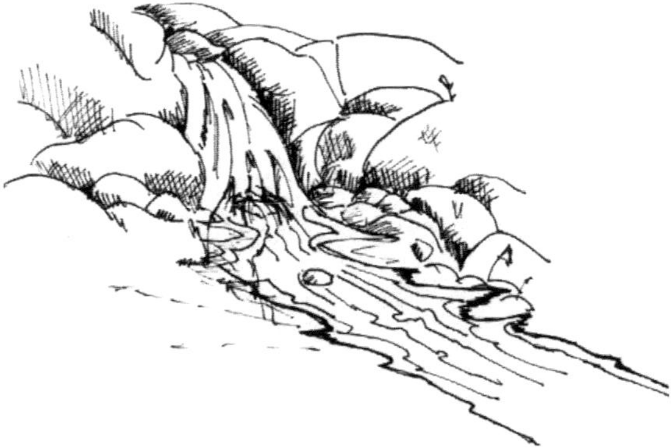

In the past, I have called the wellspring process "free-writing", "free-flow writing" or "six minute writing". We use it at the beginning of every Figment workshop.

We do so because it's essential for writers to discover that no matter how blocked or stressed you feel, your creativity can still flow – if you're willing to sit down and let it happen.

Preparation

Are you:
... sitting comfortably?
... relaxed?
... on your own (or with trusted others)?
... in a place without distractions?
... with your hand held over a blank page?

If the answer to these questions is yes, great! Ideal!

If the answer to any of these questions is no, it doesn't matter. Write anyway.

I recently found myself on a train, running late for work after bursting a tire on my car. I didn't have a notebook. So I wrote on some envelopes I found in the ticket office. When I grabbed them, the lady standing in front of me in the queue asked if I had a lot to complain about – they were supposed to be for sending complaints to Scotrail! Two short stories resulted.

The above are some guidelines for optimum writing conditions, but even if they aren't in place, you'll still be surprised by what appears on the page.

Inspiration

I highly recommend Julia Cameron's *The Artist's Way,* particularly its central practices of Morning Pages and the Artist's Date.

Cameron recommends free-writing every morning – just whatever comes to mind. While this helps writers observe what worries they repeatedly have, it didn't often, for me at least, provide the creative breakthroughs that motivate me to write. And even worse, it turned into procrastination.

In my experience, what brings people to write and what keeps them writing is the pleasure and success they experience when an idea appears

Look out the window – what's happening out there?

from nowhere. But *The Artist's Way* did help me to set up a regular practice, which in itself is invaluable.

What I discovered worked for me, and for so many other writers who've come to Figment workshops, is having a prompt to get started. The examples at the bottom of these pages are here to help you get going, and will hopefully illustrate how easy it can be to find inspiration.

If you go off topic from the original prompt, great. Anything goes.

> **Don't loaf and invite inspiration; light out after it with a club, and if you don't get it you will none the less get something that looks remarkably like it. –Jack London**

Write in key words and phrases. Sentencing and grammar will only slow you down. Don't worry about using big words. In fact, the simpler the better. This is about finding your own voice, about writing and not about trying to be a writer, whatever you think that may be. There's no need

Switch on the radio. What's the first thing that's said?

to try to be clever – being yourself is the only real way to discover what your creative voice has to offer.

Now

Set yourself a time limit – six minutes for example – and...

Go!

Don't stop, don't even hesitate, don't even think. Just write. Write as fast as you can. Write and write, even if the only things that come into your head are doubts and recriminations.

Let it Happen

Your Heckler voice will tell you that what you're writing is awful. Ignore it, and ignore it when it tells you to stop because you can't think of anything decent to write. In fact, defy it by writing down those thoughts as well! Write until your writing time is up. Then go ahead and write some more, if you like.

Remember: it's just for you. No one will read what you write unless you decide to share it.

Let whatever thoughts appear in your mind flow out through your fingers. What arrives will probably consist of random images, thoughts and memories. Nothing is irrelevant, everything has value.

Get those words down.

Eventually, after searching around with her torch for a bit, your Muse will alight on a piece of treasure and head out after it.

Think of it as a needle on a record: the music will play once you hit your groove.

I'm not asking you to write the next Man Booker Prize winner. I'm certainly not asking you to write *War and Peace* (please, don't!).

Just sit down. That's easy, isn't it? Or take a leaf out of Hemingway's book and stand up at a typewriter on a tall table.

Pick up a pen (or switch on your computer).

Open to a blank page.

Choose a prompt.

Now write. Just write for a little while, a few moments, a few minutes…

Write…

a favourite toy

There. That wasn't too bad, was it?

Now – if you've got the time and the inclination, write a bit more.

Repeat until done.

> **Exercise the writing muscle every day, even if it is only a letter, notes, a title list, a character sketch, a journal entry. Writers are like dancers, like athletes. Without that exercise, the muscles seize up. –Jane Yolen**

Don't think about the outcome, don't think too hard about planning what you'll write. Remember that if you try to control your Muse, you'll stifle her voice.

Don't let your Editor's voice drown out your Muse's whisper.

Just let it come.

Just let your thoughts appear. And if inspiration doesn't spark, write until it does.

Falkirk-based writer Helen MacKinven uses the term "freefall writing", as developed by W. O. Mitchell. In this case, it is likened to writing without a parachute. The momentum of storytelling is preserved since there's no Editor (or parachute) creating resistance for the writer with concerns about syntax and spelling.

Julia Cameron describes the process as excavating your buried dreams. Ray Bradbury likens it to opening a trapdoor into the subconscious.

Watch the "Yawp" scene from *Dead Poet's Society*. It's a miniature masterclass on stimulating the writing process.

We can all do it, and we can all find something worth yawping about. It's already there – you only need to open up to it.

Type a random letter into a search engine.

Rowing Across the Atlantic

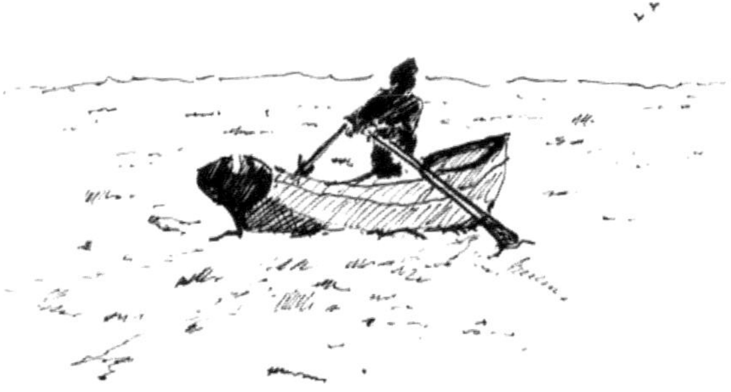

It's an overwhelming thing, the prospect of writing. We have so many dreams, so many aspirations that the prospect of actually starting becomes scary.

But… it's just a few moments.

> **Imagination is like a muscle. I found out that the more I wrote, the bigger it got. –Philip José Farmer**

As Stephen King advises, write with the door closed, edit with the door open. While you're writing, don't even think about editing or sharing your work with an audience, just revel in that afternoon, that hour, that moment you have.

Take yourself and your ambitions out of the equation – your purpose as a writer is to discover stories, give them ground to grow from, to observe them and record their movements. After that comes the editing process, but that's a job for another time and place – for now, put any thought of it off to one side.

Just write every day of your life. Read intensely. Then see what happens. Most of my friends who are put on that diet have very pleasant careers.
–Ray Bradbury

To help you put your ocean-sized ambition out of the way, inwardly trivialise what you're doing. While your ultimate ambition may be to publish an award-winning, best-selling novel, or a critically renowned collection of poetry, right now all you're doing is playing around with language to see what comes. It doesn't need to be perfect the first time. Or the second time, or the third. What you're writing now isn't the finished product.

Writing a large or a collected work is, understandably, a daunting task – especially when you get down to it and realise just how long it takes to accumulate the sheer number of words that will be your end product. Once you accept that a creative vocation is a long and evolving process, it will free you up to enjoy that journey.

Indulge yourself with over-the-top flowery language.

Writing a book is a horrible, exhausting struggle, like a long bout of some painful illness. One would never undertake such a thing if one were not driven on by some demon whom one can neither resist nor understand. –George Orwell

Look around and enjoy the scenery, rather than staring fixedly ahead at that end point. If it feels like work and nothing but work, maybe there's something wrong with your approach. So try again, try in a different way, try something new, ask new questions, go off and explore new paths. The little successes will start to happen and these will buoy you up to keep going.

A figure often thrown around is that it takes 10,000 hours of practice to become an expert. This goes back to a study done in 1993 by a professor in Colorado, and has largely been debunked, but the point remains: it takes time to master a skill.

Don't just plan to write – write. It is only by writing, not dreaming about it, that we develop our own style. –P.D. James

Writing an epic novel – or series of novels – that will end up at over 200,000 words is a huge task. No wonder it can be off-putting. Then when you factor in your Heckler who is probably telling you that it'll be a waste of time anyway because your writing will be awful and will never attract a publisher in a million years, etc. etc. etc., no wonder you're exhausted at the very thought of starting! But write a little every day, or even one day every week, and it soon starts to tot up.

> **Keep a can of WD40 on your desk – away from any open flames – to remind yourself that if you don't write daily, you will get rusty. –George Singleton**

At one hundred words a day (and that's easy – that's a tiny amount!), within two years you'll have a decent-sized novel of nearly 80,000 words on your hands. 500 words a day? There's your epic novel of nearly 200,000 words done within one year. Val MacDermid, speaking at a Bloody Scotland event, said that while working full-time, she dedicated one of her days off every week to writing. For six days, her ideas would percolate away at the back of her mind, then, on that one day, she'd spend her time getting them out of her subconscious and onto the page. This was how she wrote her first couple of novels.

If writing is what you really want to do, you can and will fit it in, no matter how busy you might consider yourself.

Stephen King, in *On Writing*, advises that all you need to write is:

- the room,
- the time,
- the determination to shut the door,
- and a concrete goal.

The longer you stick to these basics, the easier it will be for you to write. King assures writers that once you sit down and start writing, sooner or later your Muse will show up and weave her spell.

Julia Cameron describes the creative process as drawing from a well, or an "inner reservoir", and recommends that you look after this well in order to ensure it doesn't run low on ideas, or become stagnant or blocked. A regular practice is a part of this – it keeps your creative flow fresh and abundant.

What's in your pocket? (or purse, wallet or handbag)?

Echoes from the Cave

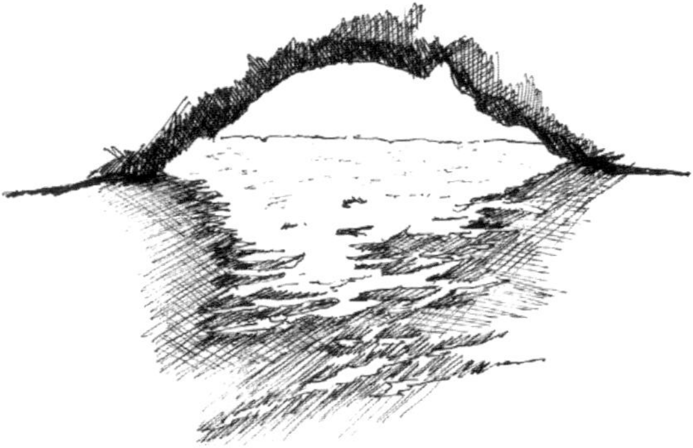

The role of a writer is not to say what we all can say, but what we are unable to say. –Anaïs Nin

By picking a writing prompt, and beginning to write from that prompt, you're asking your subconscious a question. Don't think, just let it answer.

It's funny what you think you're going to write, and then what you actually do write; it's as if something's just waiting to come up.
–Fiona Hutton, during a Figment workshop

Everyone has creative potential. You just have to allow yourself to find that potential.

I discovered that if I trusted my subconscious, or imagination, whatever you want to call it, and if I made the characters as real and honest as I could, then no matter how complex the pattern being woven, my subconscious would

If your mood were a colour, what colour would it be?

find ways to tie it together – often doing things far more complicated and sophisticated than I could with brute conscious effort. I would have ideas... story or character details... and even though I didn't quite understand, I would plunk them in. Two hundred pages later, everything would back-fit, and I'd say, "Ah, that's why I wrote that."
–Tad Williams

Structure and Flow

Some people like to plot and plan – fine, there's great comfort in that. It can also be useful to plan through a complicated novel with lots of twists and turns, secrets and reveals, flashbacks and foreshadowing. But I urge you not to constrain yourself too much during a first draft. Be brave! The adventure in writing is in the discovery when your creative flow starts and you can sit back and watch the ideas appear. If you contain your creativity in a walled-up box of plot, ideas aren't exactly going to spring forth. You may in fact discover that your best ideas are those that come freely.

It seems to me that those songs that have been any good, I have nothing much to do with the writing of them. The words have just crawled down my sleeve and come out on the page. –Joan Baez

Some people are scaffolders, and prefer to plan in detail. Other people are dreamers and like to fly by the seat of their pants, not knowing what's going to happen next. If you're a plot-driven novelist and uncomfortable without some structure, consider an approach midway between planning and pants-ing. E.L. Doctorow advises: "Writing a novel is like driving a car at night. You can only see as far as your headlights, but you can make the whole trip that way." When writing in the headlights, you might know some of the stops along the way, but you're leaving room for a few unplanned incidents on your journey. You will get more ideas as you drive, and lots of things you've only vaguely considered will be illuminated by the headlights as you get closer.

Think of it as journeying on an unknown sea at night time. By the faint light of the moon you'll see a little way ahead and you'll catch a glimpse of some twinkles of starry inspiration. Let those guide you. The adventures you observe under the surface or watch on islands as you drift along – record them. Sooner or later your story will reach land.

Looking at your Reflection in a Pool of Water
We have lots of faces we present to the world – usually the nicer faces. Your wellspring writing is a private space. You're free to let whatever comes, come, including those things that you don't usually let out to see the light of day.

> **There is nothing to writing. All you do is sit down at a typewriter and bleed. –Ernest Hemingway**

Not everything you write you'll like, or even approve of. Some of it you might be ashamed of and you'll want to throw it away. Don't. Keep it, but keep it private until you're ready to read it back over and edit it.

Writing is not a genteel profession; it's quite nasty and tough and kind of dirty. –Rosemary Mahoney

Rant, swear. Above all, let go. You'll undoubtedly be surprised by what comes. While you might not like what appears, it's no bad thing to be self-aware.

Going Fishing

Writing by using a prompt or limitation to inspire you is by no means a new technique. The Oulipo (short for the French *ouvroir de littérature potentielle* (roughly translated: "workshop of potential literature") is a group of (mainly) French-speaking writers, founded in 1960, who use constrained writing techniques to create their works. One theory is that using prompts gives the logical, problem-solving part of the mind – the same part of the mind that evaluates and edits your work – something to gnaw over. While it's distracted, your creativity is free to dart about within your subconscious and make connections.

When there's the whole world to write about, most find it difficult to know where to start. A prompt, such as those at the bottom of these pages, narrows things down, creating a funnel through which your writing can flow. All you need is a starting point to get your mind working in the way that human minds generally do: creating non-logical connections between your memories and your present moment.

It works, even for writers who initially think they'll struggle. I see that spark of inspiration light up their eyes and get to watch them find their joy in writing again.

It's that spark that keeps us going.

Sometimes "flow" or "being in the zone" feels like somebody's whispering in your ear, or moving your hand for you, or the words just appear at the front of your mind. Elizabeth Gilbert, in *Big Magic*, refers to this "most magnificent sensation imaginable" as *eudaimonia.* She explains that the ancient Greeks believed that creativity was an external force. "They didn't believe that an exceptionally gifted person was a genius; they believed that an exceptionally gifted person had a genius." When you feel that that your inspiration comes

luck

from somewhere else other than your own mind (through your Muse, Daemon, Angel, Familiar or whatever you may want to call it), it takes your ego out of the equation and helps keep narcissism at bay. It also frees you.

This creative dissociation is the same phenomenon that happens when you miss out on a conversation or part of your drive home because you've been daydreaming.

Note when flow happens and what you did to lead to it. The tips I'm sharing with you here I've learned from my own practice and from discussing the successes of many other writers, but what works is different for everyone and may be different for you at various stages in your life.

Don't be put off if your creativity doesn't spark immediately. It will, given enough of a chance.

You can't force it to happen, but you can remove obstacles that prevent it. Read on to find out how.

Imagine your Muse fishing. She will cast her line around until something bites. Let her do what she does. When inspiration bites, watch and record as your Muse reels it in.

Cloud-gaze.

The Shortest Prayer in the World

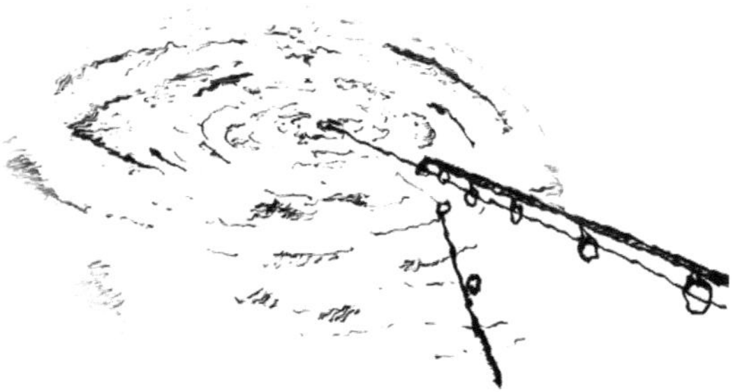

You're reading this book because you want to write, presumably. Because you love writing. But if you love writing so much, why aren't you writing all the time? Why aren't you writing now instead of reading this?

Now is not the time to be timid – you've the rest of your life for that if you choose. Now, with the blank page in front of you, now is the time to be free. So what's stopping you?

If all you do is list the reasons you're not able to get to your writing, if all you do is argue for your limitations, the less chance you'll have of getting past them.

Whatever your excuses (and I've heard and used them all), they're there for one reason and one reason only.

Fear, of course.

So what are you afraid of? Quite often, it's because writers love writing (or the idea of writing) *so* much that we're afraid of it. We're vulnerable. Most writers, coming to writing workshops for the first time, are incredibly nervous, particularly when it comes to sharing their work.

Vulnerability

The first time I went to a creative writing class, I was terrified! Running late, I found the right place, a big old council building. I skidded into a parking space, slammed the car door behind me and ran up to one of the doors, heart thumping. It was locked. I knocked. After a few moments, it swung open, and I was met by a huge force of a woman.

"HI HEN, KIN AH HELP YE?"

"Em... I'm looking for the writing class?"

"NAW, YE'VE GOTE THE WRANG PLACE!"

She shut the door in my face. I blinked and looked around. Took a step back and wondered where the hell I was going to go now.

Then the door opened again.

"ONLY KIDDIN! IN YE COME!"

Cow.

Okay, so I've not quite forgiven her yet.

I was an experienced teacher so you'd be forgiven for assuming I was full of confidence. But studying literature and teaching it to teenagers is something quite different from exposing your soul on the page.

> **Every secret of a writer's soul, every experience of his life, every quality of his mind, is written large in his works. –Virginia Woolf**

Everyone feels vulnerable when it comes to sharing their writing – even experienced writers. Exposing your soul to others is scary. Your audience will interpret your words any way they wish. They might search through it for autobiographical glimpses into your life. They might even try to psychoanalyse you. But that only happens if and when you decide to publish or perform. By that time you'll be ready for it. A good writing group will support you and prepare you.

At the wellspring stage, you don't have to worry about putting yourself out there. At that moment, your writing is just for you. There's no need to share it unless you choose to. And just in case – when you've finished your wellspring writing – hide it away somewhere nobody else will find it.

The Martyr

Sometimes we writers fall in love without even knowing it. We fall in love with a very tricky character: our Martyr. That pious voice that urges us to give up our relationship with our Muse to help everyone else. We fall so in love with earning a halo that we scrub those toilets, floors and worktops until they shine. We work overtime to fill the cupboards with food that gets thrown out, clothes we never wear and toys we distract ourselves with.

The Martyr drives us, whip cracking, to give up on our dreams until we've worked ourselves into the ground with no energy left over for writing.

Remember: you are the creator of your schedule, not the victim of it. If you really want to write, you *will* make time for it.

All of this practical stuff that the Martyr tells you that you need to do – some of it, at least, is procrastination. At the core of the Martyr is fear. Fear that you'll never be good enough.

Think about a short phrase that encapsulates your ideal life as a writer – an example from

The Artist's Way is "I am a brilliant and prolific writer". Copy out your chosen phrase ten times. As you do, be aware of what interruptions pop into your mind, perhaps from your Critic, your Heckler, your Creative or your Muse. Observe them, note them all down, and you'll see by the end just what a complex process it is to write. No wonder it's so difficult to write when we have so many voices in our heads telling us not to do it.

Make your date with your Muse and stick to it. Don't give up, don't walk away and *don't* make excuses. No writing will happen at all if the only story a writer tells is the one they tell themselves about all the reasons they can't write.

But What If...

What if you find out you can't write? What if everything you write is awful?

So what? Not everything you write will be wonderful!

> **The first draft of anything is shit.**
> **–Ernest Hemingway**

But some of what you write *will* be wonderful, and that won't appear unless you do write. There will be time in the future for editing and refinement. What you write during the wellspring process is not going to be the final product. You might not even use what you're writing now – but nothing is wasted.

The useless days... The hours writing in your journal. The long meandering walks. The hours reading poetry and story collections and novels... These things are your becoming. –Cheryl Strayed

Sometimes you have to write A to get to B. Those 200 pages of your novel back-story you're so fond of, that flash-in-the-pan description, written so artfully, that just doesn't fit no matter how hard you try to crowbar it in – those might well have to go.

Murder your darlings, as Sir Arthur Quiller-Couch said. Sometimes it's your fondest turns of phrase that unfortunately need to be cut. But all that writing hasn't been a waste of time, I assure you. The best way to write and keep writing is to fall in love with the writing process, not with the outcome.

What if what you write isn't instantly perfect? Unfortunately, you're entering into a community full of perfectionists. No writer is ever satisfied with what they've done. What comes out on the page will only very rarely look as good as what you first imagined.

When I write, I feel like an armless, legless man with a crayon in his mouth. –Kurt Vonnegut

You may feel like a fraud. All writers feel like frauds at some point – but nobody can tell your story the way you can. Measure your success as a writer by your dedication, not by what you produce.

What if you feel like you don't have enough experience? Don't worry: you'll gain experience as you go along. You already have loads of experience to draw on – perhaps not of writing or of publishing, but of life – and that, after all, is what you're writing about. Ignore that inner voice that tells you that you know nothing. That you haven't led an exciting enough life to have anything worthwhile to contribute. This is simply not true.

> **Anyone who is going to be a writer knows enough at fifteen to write several novels. –May Sarton**

Are you worried you don't know enough about the technicalities of style? Here's another secret: overusing these linguistic techniques can result in stories and poetry that's overwrought, self-conscious and pretentious. Writing like this doesn't ring true. It feels stilted.

Better to write simply. It's through simplicity that the truth, *your* truth, shines. A clear window reveals a view far better than stained glass.

Stylistic techniques can, of course, be used to polish writing, but you learn how to use these tools as you go (and often most effectively through discussion or reading). While writing, and particularly while editing, you instinctively make decisions about what words to use and in what order. And what words not to use.

Reading as a writer becomes a more critical (and I mean that in a positive sense) and engaging process. Some wondrous word in the right place (or phrase, or sentence, or paragraph) will sing to you, and you'll stop to consider what it was about the word choice and structure that made it so effective. Often, it's a case of instinct. Trust your instincts. When it's right, it'll chime with something deep inside you.

If you still think anything you write right now will be awful – go away and try!

You never know, you might surprise yourself.

What's the worst thing that could happen?

> **Everything in life is writable about if you have the outgoing guts to do it, and the imagination to improvise. The worst enemy to creativity is self-doubt. –Sylvia Plath**

What if someone doesn't like your work? That's their choice. Write anyway. When you decide to publish your work, it will find its audience. Even if it's an intimate audience of friends and family, it will be cherished and valued. But that's for another day.

What if someone criticises your work at a workshop? That's why you're there! Of course, sometimes people could give their criticism more gently, and not all criticism is well-intended, but you can always learn from it. Without it, you can't improve – whether that's as a result of listening to and following their advice, or listening and then dismissing their opinions – it all helps to streamline your writing and your individual voice.

Are you worried you might write something that others will be offended by? You don't need to publish everything you write, and you should definitely edit your work before publishing it to wipe away anything that may get you into trouble. These are things that can all be dealt with in the future. For the moment – just write.

When it comes down to it, you're on your own. Your writing group, your nearest and dearest, all can give you advice – that doesn't mean it's necessarily right or even helpful. Your responsibility is to your writing, because you're the one who cares the most for it. Nurture it because nobody else will.

Stop complaining, stop making excuses and use that energy to write instead.

So – what's the shortest prayer in the world?

"F**k it."

F**k the fear and write anyway.

The Critic and the Creative

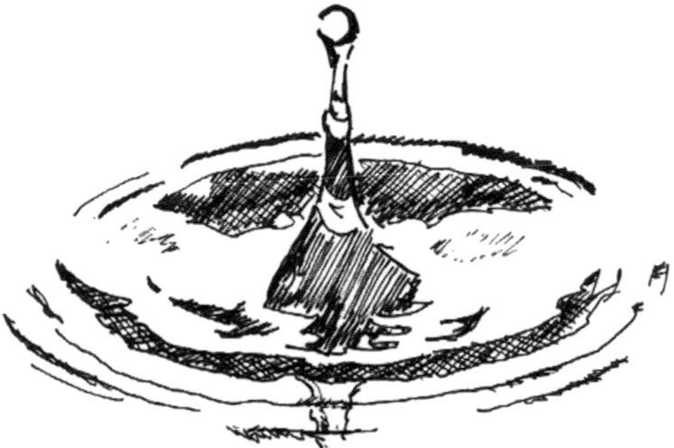

Good writing is about exploring your humanity. That common humanity will hit a nerve with others, too. "Let the world burn through you," advises Ray Bradbury in *Zen in the Art of Writing*. A writer is a prism for light to shine through. Every different writer diffracts that light in a completely unique way, but one thing that stops this from happening is our critical voice.

Your Creative is a sensitive soul. Your Critic, on the other hand is a perfectionist. He means well. While the Creative wants to have fun, the Critic wants us to be the best we can be. But he can also be a bit of a bully.

My Critic is called Shirley. She's an over-processed bleached blonde with skin petrified like tree bark that's been out in the sun too long. She has long, taloned nails with chipped pink varnish and blows smoke drawn from cigarettes she holds like Cruella de Vil.

Shirley doesn't have much patience for the Creative's relationship with the Muse. She considers it a fun but essentially massive waste of valuable time. So a fair chunk of my writing process has been learning how to nudge Shirley off to one side and let my Muse through. Likewise, a great deal of my time as a writing tutor is spent identifying the voices of other writers' Critics and helping those writers find strategies to work around them.

What you write doesn't have to be perfect the first time, or the second, or the third time. Rebecca Solnit counsels that the perfect is the enemy of the good, the realistic, the possible and the fun.

> **Literature is strewn with the wreckage of men who have minded beyond reason the opinions of others.**
> **–Virginia Woolf**

Don't allow yourself to be stopped in your tracks by a detail that niggles you as you write it. Editing as you go along disrupts your flow and invites the Critic in. I advise that if you must concede to your inner Editor just a little, only concede so far as to underline or highlight or annotate at the side what you know you'll want to go back and change. Then you can shut the door on your Critic and enjoy your writing time in peace.

All writers have different processes. Some writers break their days into word counts: Ian McEwan writes a minimum of 500 words a day. Jack London and George Bernard Shaw wrote at least 1,000 words a day, while Thomas Wolfe wrote 10,000 words a day! At the other end of the spectrum are equally wonderful writers like Janice Galloway, who feels glad to have written a paragraph a day. These are painstaking literary first-draft perfectionists. James Joyce was happy if he wrote a few sentences each day. (Mind you, when you see the length of some of Joyce's sentences...)

Wellspring writing doesn't necessarily work for every writer. Some writers prefer to edit as they go, painstakingly considering every single word and its placement before moving on. A famous conversation with Joyce went something like this:

"I've been working hard on [Ulysses] all day," said Joyce.

"Does that mean you've written a great deal?"

"Two sentences," said Joyce... "I have the words already. What I am seeking is the perfect order of words in the sentence."

The main advantage of this way of writing, I suppose, is that the editing process takes less time. There's no right or wrong here – everyone works in their own way.

For those who are starting out or for writers who have stalled, I maintain that writing quickly without thinking is the way to go. During that first drafting process, your goal is just to get the words down. Ray Bradbury advises that "in quickness is truth." I've tried writing in various different ways, and writing quickly in response to a random prompt helps to get my ideas flowing like nothing else. That doesn't mean you need to write furiously; sometimes slow and steady is the way to go, as long as you don't stop.

One thing that helps is to give myself permission to write badly. I tell myself that I'm going to do my five or ten pages no matter what, and that I can always tear them up the following morning if I want. I'll have lost nothing-writing and tearing up five pages would leave me no further behind than if I took the day off.
–Lawrence Block

Write a letter to your past self.

You may have dreams of becoming an award-winning, best-selling author some day, and cringe whenever you write something that doesn't measure up to your expectations, but it's important to get that ego-drive out of the way while you're writing. What you write may not end up being what you intended, but does that really matter? It's certainly better than a blank page!

Stephen King describes writing as archaeology, a process of discovery. I prefer to think of it as a sculpture. Writing your first draft is a quick and dirty process of hacking a big hunk of rock from a cliff-face. Your story, script or poem is in there, and the chunk of rock you have at that moment will be the rough shape of the finished product. Then, during each stage of editing, you use finer and finer tools, chipping away and filing down any rough edges – characters, chapters, pages, paragraphs, sentences, phrases and words. You dust and polish away small errors – giving it the care and attention it deserves, until finally you have a polished, shining work of art before you. But first – you need something to work with. So stand at that rock face, hammer and chisel in hand, and get started.

Finding Your Wings

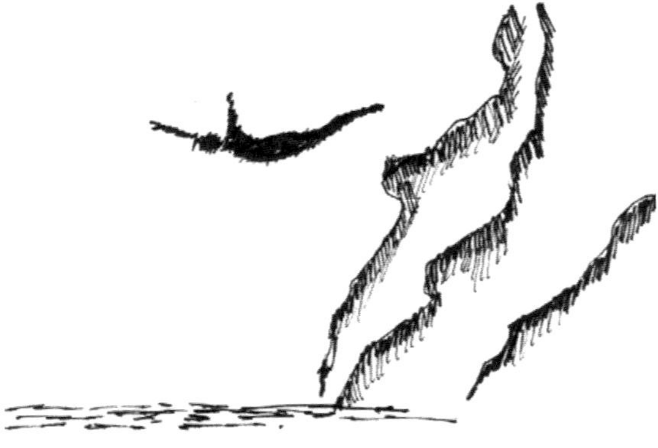

You can, you should, and if you're brave enough to start, you will.
–Stephen King

No matter how fearless you are in the rest of your life, if you're "blocked" with your writing, fear is at the bottom of it.

There's no such thing as writer's block. That was invented by people in California who couldn't write.
–Terry Pratchett

You could spend a fortune on writing guides, on software, on tools and books full of advice and prompts. You could spend time planning out your epic novel, on research, on reading novels, stories, poetry and creative non-fiction. You could go to writing classes, workshops, courses, and retreats. You could learn all about other writers and their processes and writing spaces and routines.

These practices all have their use, but can also become procrastination. Ultimately, (as I tell the writers at my workshops), none of this will make you a better writer unless you actually write!

The art of writing is the art of applying the seat of the pants to the seat of the chair. –Mary Heaton Vorse

One advantage of a good writing class is that the desire to write creatively is taken seriously. In a group of fellow writers, you'll find the kindred spirits you've been looking for all your life who actually understand. They won't look at you in bafflement as well-meaning family or friends may, nor will they scorn or pity you, as some unimaginative or repressed individuals may. Your writing comrades will encourage and join you as you explore your inner landscapes. A good writing group will celebrate and support your discoveries. That support can be key to maintaining your motivation – and to giving you a gentle kick up the bottom when necessary.

Not My Circus, Not My Monkeys

Some days, we hope that someone else will come in to take control of our life, and put it back in order. Is that why you're reading this book?

Sorry, but nobody's going to be your ringmaster – myself included.

Ultimately, it's up to you to write. It's your circus, your monkeys, and you *can* harness them. Realise that your Instant Gratification Monkeys want to divert you away into doing something that has an instant pay-off. That's your procrastination talking. And at the bottom of that is fear.

If you write, even a little at a time, you *will* discover something that makes it all worth it. Use your temptations to motivate you. Once you do a certain amount of writing, then you can go play – if you want to. You may end up having so much fun writing that you won't want to do anything else You can rejoin the circus of your life any time that you choose. For this moment, you are choosing to write.

Don't be "A Writer"

Some people like the idea of being a writer more than they actually like to write. Quite a few, actually!

People on the outside think there's something magical about writing, that you go up in the attic at midnight and cast the bones and come down in the morning with a story, but it isn't like that. You sit in back of the typewriter and you work, and that's all there is to it. –Harlan Ellison

Writing may not end up being for you, and that's okay. But in order to find that out, to make sure you don't live out your life with that lingering *what if?*, you're going to have to give it a go.

Get it down. Take chances. It may be bad, but it's the only way you can do anything really good.
–William Faulkner

If you want to be a writer – write. Don't find the time, *make* the time. Value it, treasure it and protect it.

No amount of self-inflicted misery, altered states, black pullovers or being publicly obnoxious will ever add up to your being a writer. Writers write. On you go. –A.L. Kennedy

Courage, Tenacity and Risk

A professional writer is an amateur who didn't quit. –Richard Bach

I won't guarantee that wellspring writing will always be easy. What will make you a writer is writing even when it's not all sunshine and smiles and free-flowing water. Your endurance will be tested, your stamina, your nerve. And when you feel the most frustrated and fearful – that's probably when you're about to experience a big breakthrough. So when things get difficult, stick with it. The biggest difference between a successful writer and an unsuccessful writer is tenacity. So go forth and write.

Whatever you can do, or dream you can do, begin it. Boldness has genius, power and magic in it.
–Johann Wolfgang von Goethe

At Some Point, You Just Have to Jump

Having said all of this, you could be forgiven for assuming I don't sympathise with the plight of the stuck writer. I do, I really do!

It takes guts to be a writer – more guts than it takes to jump out of a plane. Trust me, I used to throw myself out of planes as a hobby.

The most frightening part of parachuting is the approach. It's getting into the plane, waiting for it to circle round high enough to your jump-point. It's sitting on the edge of that open hatch.

The scariest moment is always just before you start. –Stephen King

Once you decide there's no going back, that the only way forward is to jump, you experience pure freedom.

That moment when you push yourself out into the air? There's nothing like it. Exhilarating.

What happens afterwards, well – you'll find out.

We have to continually be jumping off cliffs and developing our wings on the way down. –Kurt Vonnegut

Over the Rainbow

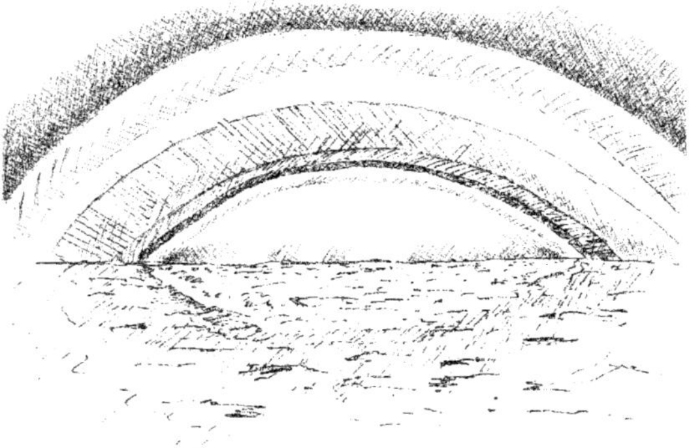

For a rainbow to exist, there needs to be both rain and sunshine.

> **Every writer I know has trouble writing. –Joseph Heller**

We can do this the easy way, or...

Sorry – but there's no easy way to be a successful writer, whatever you imagine that may be. Writing is lonely work. It's a slog – novel writing especially.

> **I love being a writer. What I can't stand is the paperwork.**
> **–Peter De Vries**

This is where wellspring writing comes in. It reminds you that no matter how rough a spell of writing you're going through, you can still enjoy that buzz of inspiration. It reminds you that the sun *will* break through the clouds if you let it.

Remember you love writing. It wouldn't be worth it if you didn't. If the love fades, do what you need to and get it back. –A.L. Kennedy

That flow is the writer's addiction. It's what we crave even more than the success of connection with our audience. It will carry you on past the shallows of creative dearth.

What the writer probably needs most is an almost daemonic compulsiveness. –John Gardner

Sometimes the flow doesn't happen. Sometimes you sit down and you feel like you have to crank your writing out. Every. Single. Word. Still, sit down and write. Flow happens eventually, you just have to give yourself the chance. Don't worry, inspiration will flow again.

There is no rule on how to write. Sometimes it comes easily and perfectly; sometimes it's like drilling rock and then blasting it out with charges. –Ernest Hemingway

Expecting to find the end of a rainbow is pretty daft. I found that out, to my eternal disappointment, when I was five years old, and went off on that particular hunt on my own (much to my mother's consternation).

That doesn't mean it's not fun to try. Wellspring writing is a tool to help you on your way. The adventure has its own rewards.

> **It's in the doing that the idea comes.**
> **–Edmund Bacon**

If you want to write, but don't know if you're able to, I'm afraid there's only one way to find out. Don't plan and plan your novel without actually starting it. You'll get your best ideas while actually writing.

> **Start writing, no matter what. The water does not flow until the faucet is turned on. –Louis L'Amour**

If you don't set out on your own hero's journey, you'll never find out what you're capable of, you'll never find out what you really think and you'll never find out who you really are.

Writing is all about setting off on a path of discovery. Writing helps muddy ideas settle into clarity. Often, I'll write in order to work out my thoughts and feelings over some issue that's niggling me. Sometimes I don't even know what I think, deep down, until I see it there on the page.

> **I write because I don't know what**
> **I think until I read what I say.**
> **–Flannery O'Connor**

When you write creatively, you'll uncover knowledge you didn't even realise you knew. Solutions to that plot you've been wrangling with will suddenly just appear. Ideas will come from a place that you know isn't inside you, it's from somewhere much more mysterious. That's the real stuff of writing. For that, you need to connect with your subconscious, your Muse.

> **I couldn't wait to get to work in the morning: I wanted to know what I was going to say.**
> **–Sharon O'Brien**

I don't believe in writers' blocks. I believe in fear. You'll never lose it, nor should you. Don't fight it, accept it. Never grow complacent over your writing.

Fear is what makes you human. It's what makes your writing human. Just please don't let it stop you.

Setting Off

> **This is how you do it: you sit down at the keyboard and you put one word after another until it's done. It's that easy, and that hard. –Neil Gaiman**

Water is a vastly powerful force, as is creativity. Once you start writing, your creativity can flow around, over, and even through your fear, just as water always finds a way around, over or through any obstacle, given time.

Your writing won't flow until you open yourself, even a tiny chink of yourself, to the infinite depths of your own creativity.

You can do it. So stop reading this and go do some writing.

Six minutes, starting.... now!

Showcase

Frances Ainslie: Free-writing is exciting. It's like unlocking the cage of your subconscious and setting images and words free. Often what comes fluttering out will surprise you. Never underestimate the beauty of the creativity that's locked deep inside. It's a great way to unblock your inspiration when you've become stuck with your writing. It's a bit like in the film *Billy Elliot*, where the examiner asks him what it feels like when he's dancing, and he says, "... I forget everything ... I feel a change in my whole body ... I'm just there. Flyin'."

The Scent of Words

I cajole the groaning door open and the smell wraps itself around me. It's an odd smell; a mixture of old tobacco, dust and tears. In the silence my eyes close as if by rote. I should open the wooden shutters and let the autumn light stutter into the dark room where the oak shelves are crammed with antique books covered in aged vellum and dark leather. My hand rests on the fissured surface of the reading desk feeling history seep through my fingertips.

Over three hundred years and nothing has changed.

I am encased in a nutshell.

It is nine minutes past opening time. I should free the latch on the window shutters but I'm dreaming, floating upwards to the highest shelf captured in a musty spore of time. What if today, it's only me and the books?

In the stillness I fancy I hear a bookworm threading through labyrinths of tiny holes on page thirty-four of Adam Smith's *Wealth of Nations*.

Across the street a blackbird tells his story to the sky.

I move to the window, raise the latch, and throw back both shutters with an ear-shattering clatter. Sunlight rushes in to meet me stirring dust motes to send them spiralling to find a hiding place. Some settle on the tops of presses while others cling to the delicate spider web embroidered between the arms of the chandelier. The book shelves relax when illuminated, weeping beeswax from their hand-dowelled corners. I gently lift Buffon's *Histoire Naturelle* and a pale yellow moth flutters to the floor flat as a pressed flower. My breath catches as Lady Jane Grey's

Prayer Book slumps forward on the shelf as if mourning the loss, her gold-etched spine glittering in a dart of sunlight. Fifty minutes gone with no visitors. This is the way it should be. Just me, and the books, cocooned from the outside world. The only sound the whisper of a turning page. Sometimes I read a book out loud to hear the soft echo of the words soar upwards to the galleried ceiling. But mostly I'm content to listen to the library's under-song. I drift through time touched by the voices of scholars, travellers, preachers, artists, dreamers – their life of words congregated here in this special place.

The oldest book is a 1504 *Book of Psalms* written in Latin. It lies open under glass; the Bishop's spidery handwriting barely visible in the margins, faded violet blue by centuries of candle-light. Touching the ink I've a notion that I can sense him from the page. I wonder if his life would have been bearable without his books and dreams.

Outside, life goes on. The red maple scatters leaves in the manse garden. A dog barks by the river. Walking home I can still smell the breath of the library on my clothes, the words in my mouth, and that strange papery taste on my tongue.

That's the way it is. Nothing changes there.

The sense of smell is often neglected in writing – but it is wonderfully evocative. Use an example of smell to start you off. You'll be surprised by how sensory your writing can become, as well as the memories that surface.

Rosie Brown: I would never have been able to switch my inner critic off enough for free writing in my normal life. But my youngest child is a poor sleeper and I have spent countless hours of my life sitting quietly in the darkness beside a cot or bed. I keep a notebook and pencil under the bed, and slide down to get my arm underneath and scribble. I move things out that have been clogging up my brain, and often see a new insight on a problem. Sometimes the writing becomes a poem or a story, or a snippet of something bigger. Sometimes I can't read it. There's a peculiar freedom to writing words you can't see in the dark.

Count With Baby

You should put a clock
In the baby's room.
One you can read in the nearly-dark
to know if you are missing something
or if you are missed.
It may be twenty to
but that could be the hour hand
you can count their breath
one, two, three...
Five is nothing
five is just a pause between cries
pay no attention to five

Lie down.
Six, seven, eight...
wait
Oh, God
oh, nine, ten
ten is good.
No, lie down

Do not let yourself hope at fifteen
sixteen, seventeen...
At twenty you may hope.
No, we are not beeping noses.
No.
One, two, three...
No, we are going to sleep

If you close your eyes
she may take the hint
fourteen, fifteen…
No, that was just daddy
Bad daddy
Lie down darling

At thirty, things look good
Thirty-four, thirty-five..
breath a little slower
you may start to move
one milimeter per count is best
glance through your eyelashes:
oh! She looks back, wondering

thirty-nine, forty..
strange they don't hear
your muscles scream
Do not!
take your weight too quickly off the cot
it may creak you back to
one, two, three…

forty-six, forty-seven, forty-eight
it may be easier to crawl
out of the room.
you are not free until the door hisses shut

it must've been the hour hand

Your energy at different times of day can create different resonances with your writing. Try well-spring writing as soon as you wake up, in the middle of the night if you can't sleep, at midday, before you go to sleep, and so on, to see how it affects your creative output.

Norma Austin Hart: I am very good at talking about writing, going on courses, reading and doing exercises, researching my ideas – anything to avoid actually writing. The Figment workshops helped me work out what I need to do to be creative, and the most important element of that is to sit down every day and write for at least six minutes. Put like that it sounds achievable and I believe that is why it works. Often I write for longer, and sometimes the ideas that spill out become something more substantial in my imagination. Something I can work with.

The Grocer's Shop

My dad says the customers are good for us. They want to spend money in our shop so I have to be nice to them. I don't always want to be nice to them, 'specially when I stick my fingers in a rotten potato and the smell stays under my nails. Dad says I should wash my hands but I don't like to. It's too far to walk to the stone sink in the cold lobby at the back door. I burned my leg once with the steam from the kettle that sits by the stone sink. I have the scar on my leg now.

I like the feel of the furry tomatoes and I like rubbing the apples on my apron and putting the shiny ones at the front of my display. Four of them go into the brown bag nicely and I can spin it around twice and the bag doesn't split. When it's not busy I write the price on the bag with my dad's pen. In the morning when we start I go through all the fruit and vegetables in the window and take out the rotten bruised ones. Dad says if I think they are not too bad I can make them "special offer of the day", and I make a sign with the price. He has shown me how to draw the numbers so they look grown up and I can colour them with different marker pens. Then I have to pile up the oranges and turnips so they look "appealing" my granny says.

"Appealing" is hard. I know they have to look clean and fresh so I try for rows and pyramids. Then when someone wants to buy some I don't want to sell them. Sometimes I say, "Are you sure?"

When Mrs Black comes in she sometimes asks me for the throw away potatoes. Once I saw her put some apples in her pocket. My granny says she is feckless. I don't know what feck is but Mrs Black doesn't have any and she is in the tick book. She is tickful. Maybe feck is money because she doesn't ever have any. My dad sometimes gives me potatoes to put in a bag for her when he sees her walking towards the shop.

Mrs Gordon comes in shouting because she likes a drink. I know the drink is sherry but I don't understand why she shouts sometimes and other times cries.

I love it when wellspring writing uncovers a memory we thought we'd long forgotten. This was one such example, written by Norma during a workshop. Consider an important place from your childhood, the things that happened there, the people you encountered.

Sally Evans: A good poem's inspiration often comes while you are actually writing – you suddenly see your way somewhere, go with the words, and discard what you had written before. It can just be anything you notice or that occurs to you, to ease you into writing. With experiencc you do not tussle with syntax and connections.

For Clara

I sit writing with Ann's daughter Clara,
In the wide sunny room, she on her iPad,
I with the old pen & ink. Quiet prevails
and it strikes me how odd, for her,
to have an aunt who's a poet.

When we stop in the end, she says
did I wrote a poem?
yes I say, thinking two, the second useful
the first an exercise.
I say I began by freewriting.

We talk about houses.
She says in which house *Jane Eyre* is set.
We talk about Jane Eyre houses
(an orchard and two staircases),
while Charlotte Brontë hovers in the wings.

I love a bit of writing about writing. Free writing about the processes and challenges and passions of writing can be a great tool to use to help motivate yourself.

Duncan Carmichael: I found that the secret was to grab an idea and run with it, no matter how unlikely or ridiculous it seemed. Until I realised that, I was paralysed by trying to stick to "the subject". It was when I realised the subject was essentially meaningless that I started to write things that I thought might be of use, or could be developed.

The best pieces of writing that have come out of six minute writing feel more like I'm reading the story than writing it. It's completely effortless, other than the pain in my hand from writing so fast.

Sunflower Oil

It didn't take him long to realise that slicking his hair back with sunflower oil was a terrible idea. Barely a hundred yards from the house, the flies started to congregate around him and by the time he reached Janis's house there was an actual cloud of them buzzing and thrumming around him. He ran the last hundred yards, and knocked frantically at the door, willing her to open it before they caught him.

Her timing couldn't have been any worse. She opened the door precisely at the moment the cloud arrived, and John tumbled in followed by an entire cloud of frenzied buzzing insects. She screamed as the hall turned black with them, landing on her face and her hair and all around her, inside her ears. One flew straight into her mouth and her face twisted as she realised she'd swallowed it.

Afraid of the Dark

Dennis was afraid of the dark. At least, that's what he told his Mum. He didn't want her to find out what he was really afraid of, so he told her he was afraid of the dark every time he went to bed. She was kind and understanding, so she didn't make a fuss, just put on his night light, gave him a kiss and left him to get on with things.

That's when it would appear. At first it had appeared at the window, and he'd tried to ignore it, tap tap tapping on the glass, but eventually he'd given in and opened the window. It had leapt straight in and scurried across the floor and under the bedclothes, shivering and groaning. He'd tried to budge it, but it clung fiercely to the headboard screaming as if he was torturing it, until eventually he'd given up and left it alone. He slept on the floor that night, and every night since. What Dennis was most afraid of was his Mum finding it in his room.

Ninjas

Ninjas. That was the name of the coffee shop we'd agreed to meet in. The name hinted of many things, probably none of those intended by the owners. I suspected the owners were youngish, say around 30, probably male and bearded with the latest in cool clothing and a line of coffees designed to "kick your taste buds into the 21st century". Or "subtle flavours that sneak up and knife you in the back before you even know they're there". That's what they'd want you to believe, but what I imagined was a ridiculously overpriced, trendy, hipster fad coffee bar with jam jars for coffee cups and old Frisbees for plates.

The reality was the delightful opposite. A grumpy old Asian man stood glowering at me as I tried to decide between a black or white coffee, cleaning out a cup with a dirty old tea towel.

"What you want?" he demanded, and I grinned despite myself. It was all I could do not to hug him.

Duncan's examples of wellspring writing give a brilliant indication of just how varied a writer's work can be. If you feel your work is getting a bit same-y and stale, push out of your comfort zone by trying a completely new type of prompt, or even experiment with a new genre. Write fearlessly.

Rachel Kay: I always seem to reach my stride at the three-minute mark. From almost nothing, words build towards a crescendo, ideas connecting themselves...

Purple

The colour of nearly-frozen fingertips, clenched hand-in-hand, a child's scrunched-up face, bawling. The indiscriminate middle-ground between boy and girl.

The colour of royalty, of a wine stain, or a really good sunset.

Of the violets in our garden, freckled with black, that my mum said were good luck and cheered her up when Dad left. After he was gone, she painted the whole house purple.

The colour of blackberries fattening in their thicket of thorns, staining our palms as we checked for tiny bugs inside.

Of the passion flowers that climbed the screen on my window, and the deep, howling darkness during a thunder storm – the clouds mauve and the sky almost yellow, like a bruise.

The colour of a scar, nearly healed, darkening under a roasting shower. Revealing the rest of the story like invisible ink.

Before the Snow

When the air is crisp with that snow smell, taut with expectation like the canopy of a blanket fort constructed between sofa cushions and inspiring the same childish glee.

Before that first flake touches its feathery edge to the earth, before the trees put on their party clothes and drifts mound up in the fields, at this moment the season is laden with possibilities. With perfection and freshness. An idealism that ends with the first footfall into its untrodden whiteness.

Soon it will soften, become pock-marked with raindrops and sludgey with mud, forming icy puddles that trickle away into gutters.

But for now, as an idea, a promise cradled by clouds and held in the sky, that first snowfall remains flawless.

These are fabulous examples of how one tiny concept can be expanded. I'm often impressed by how well my writers use a short, specific space of time to write a complete, rounded-off piece. It's amazing, too, how such diverse pieces can be produced from the same prompt. Writing flash fiction is a difficult task. Giving yourself a specific amount of time can be surprisingly helpful.

Fiona Hutton: I have loved what free-writing enables me to do. The permission to write without unattainable perfection, to allow thoughts to come up to the surface and grant them their voice. I especially appreciate how this process allows me to unearth treasures that I would have otherwise struggled to find. I recall how uncharacteristically peaceful and calm I felt while writing this short piece. It enabled me to honestly acknowledge the gifts whilst also honouring my losses.

Beginning

Beginning is such a special word because it can mean just that. A beginning, the start of something new or it can also be a beginning as a result of an ending. I've had lots of new beginnings in my life, sometimes just through the natural process of life and some not so natural. Abrupt, sudden beginnings from endings, difficult and challenging.

Equally, beginnings have brought me new steps in my life, a relief to be past a difficult time but it's not linear. Sometimes two steps forwards and six steps back but always feeling more relieved for these beginnings when I see and feel the growth that's occurred. Beginnings, new life, new opportunities, blessings, gifts and lessons learned.

Sometimes wellspring writing can provide a starting point for larger work. There are numerous such examples in here of things that Fiona could take forward and write about in greater depth. Do the same now – look over your previous examples and take a seed of an idea from one that, with a bit of nurturing, has the potential to grow into something larger. Use it as your prompt.

Janet Crawford: I wrote this poem a few months back in 10 mins, but it was rumbling around in my head before this and kept surfacing as I worked. I can often have a line repeat itself in my head and then one or two words being added appears to be the catalyst for writing that I need at that time. I try to allow each poem to develop itself and I'm aware that whilst much of my work may be unstructured and technically poor, I am more interested in developing my own "writing voice" currently, and I hope to develop my work technically as I improve and spend time around more experienced poets. I'm lucky that I can adopt a fairly relaxed mindset whilst working, and this has helped me immensely.

HEART-BEAT

ONE BEAT, TWO BEATS, THREE BEATS,
FOUR
One Beat, Two Beats, Three Beats, Four
one beat, two beats, thre.....

No DNR sign required
As the life's long since expired
The career I thought defined me
Flatlined _________________,
and is no more

I watched on as I floundered and
gasped
my last
breaths
After
A lifetime
In nursing, this
was the last
Test

No longer able to identify with what
I thought made me, 'ME'....
I resigned, adjusted my thinking and set myself
FREE.

Ideas often percolate away at the back of your mind. wellspring writing lets these break through to the light of day. Sometimes it's a good idea to give yourself a prompt and let it bubble away in your subconscious for a few hours, even days, before writing.

Ailie Wallace: I love free-writing as an exercise as it's a great way to just let your pen flow. I usually do it as a warm-up in the morning to get into a creative mindset. I never throw any of it away – I always hang on to it in case I can somehow work it into a larger piece. Occasionally I'm able to produce an entire stand-alone poem or piece of fiction within a five or six-minute time frame.

Regret

It's coloured red, like a big bright warning
reminding me of what I've done.
It smells like fish,

impossible to diffuse or escape.
Its jagged texture prods deep,
scratching into my soul.
A constant buzz in my ears,
that only I can hear.
A blizzard of confusion which
leaves me disoriented and alone.
It follows me around for weeks, months;
like a lap-dog it never leaves my side.
It stands over me like a mountain
which I must one day conquer
in order to be free.

Ailie wrote this poem during a Figment workshop in response to a synaesthesia style prompt. Try giving an abstract noun (such as an emotion) colours, smells, textures, and sounds.

Kirstine Sloan: Six-minute writing? Great for letting ideas and thoughts from the subconscious bubble to the surface. You surprise yourself with the words that end up on the page!

Unbroken Chain
Since the days of Rapunzel
Women have understood
the power of a long, twisted braid
Needing no rescue
and no permanent waves
it was a woman
who discovered the pattern of Double Helix
The twisting curve of fate
nature's predetermined sway
Never credited but nonetheless
A credit to us all

I saw the link first hand,
when genes go awry
What havoc they reap!
Despair call forth
To be aided not by medication or science or the
healer:
those fops that conceal the true nature of disease
But by loving arms who picked her up and shook
her roughly 'til she laughed

> ***Fairy tales from our childhood influence our writing and subconscious in ways we can't begin to describe. Use these to tap into your wellspring.***

Acknowledgements and Contributors

Frances Ainslie lives in Dunblane. She kick-started her writing journey in 2013 by attending a Figment Creativity writing class and graduated with an MLitt in Creative Writing in 2015. Frances writes fiction, creative non-fiction and poetry with works published in various anthologies and magazines: most recently, the Scottish Book Trust's *Secrets & Confessions*, launched for Book Week Scotland 2016.

Rachel Kay has just finished an MLitt in Publishing at the University of Stirling. Her first professional project has been to edit and produce this book. Growing up in Florida and Italy with her unconventional family has provided plenty of material for her writing, and she is regularly distracted by the gorgeous Scottish landscape whilst trying to drive.

Rosie Brown was born and brought up in nearly Northwest England but has lived in Scotland for so long now that she can say "aye, right" without feeling self conscious at all. Once, when she was 18, she lied and told everyone it was her birthday so that they would be nice to her. It worked! They even bought her a cake. She has worked as lots of peculiar things, including a teacher of circus skills, a massage therapist, a scriptwriter, and a TV researcher. Those things were fun, but all the time she suffered from an uncontrollable urge to make up stories. She was probably just hoping for more cake. She lives in central Scotland with a husband, a dog, and two children (who she hopes will never lie about their birthdays).

Ann Shaw, formerly a journalist for *The Herald*, graduated from Glasgow School of Art in 2001. She now works as a freelance artist/writer, and is a founding member of Forth Valley Open Studios. Ann is an environmental campaigner, on the board of Creative Stirling, and has published two books, *The Children of Craig-y-nos* (co-authored with Dr. Carole Reeves) and *Paolozzi Revealed.* She can be found online at www.annshaw.co.uk.

Sally Evans has published several books of poetry, both in print and on Kindle, plus innumerable poems. She edits the *Poetry Scotland* broadsheet. Sally lives in Callander, near Stirling.

Ailie Wallace is a creative writer from Falkirk, who is currently on a maternity break from her day-job as a freelance writer. She was recently published in the *Secrets & Confessions* anthology for Book Week Scotland, and is also working on a novel.

Duncan Carmichael is a creative accountant and inveterate dabbler who lives by the mantra, "there must be an easier way than this." His love of books is surpassed only by his feverish passion for Microsoft Excel.

Helen MacKinven writes contemporary Scottish fiction and is the author of the novels *Talk of the Toun* and *Buy Buy Baby.* She has an MLitt in Creative Writing from the University of Stirling, and her short stories have appeared in a number of literary anthologies and journals, such as *Gutter* magazine.

Fiona Hutton from Wallacestone is enjoying her first experience of creative writing during a career break caring for her family. She is especially interested in personal and therapeutic writing, and enjoys writing poems. Her Facebook posts, detailing the impacts of family life living with M.S., were featured in the *Falkirk Herald* newspaper during M.S. Awareness Week.

Janet Crawford is a Larbert-based writer and has been writing since 2014. She writes mostly poetry. Published works have appeared in the following: *Untitled V & VII*; *The Write Angle*; various fanzines; *The Steamie* by Govanhill Baths Community Trust; *Anti-Heroin Chic*. Janet is a member of F.W.S., Rooftop Writers, and the Forth Valley Writers' Collective.

Kirstine Sloane lives in Alloa and is a member of the Alloa Writers' Group and Resonate. She was inspired by a short course at Moniak Mhor, her association with the W.E.A., and by Figment. Experimenting with short stories and poems, she hopes to find her authentic voice and to keep developing her skills in creative writing.

Rosa Macpherson is a writer of short stories, poetry, and social history articles. She received her Master of Art in Creative Writing at Napier, writing crime fiction. Her work appears in various editions of *New Writing Scotland*, *Edinburgh Review*, *Collins Short Stories*, *The Devil & The Giro*, and publications in the U.S. and Ireland.

Norma Austin Hart is a writer based in Edinburgh and studying for an MLitt in Creative Writing at the University of Stirling. She has written and produced a play at the Edinburgh Festival Fringe called *G-L-O-R-I-A!* and is also published as a short story writer by the Scottish Book Trust.

John McHarg is an artist and illustrator who grew up in the East End of Glasgow. He studied Art and Design at Cardonald College, Spatial Design at Glasgow College of Building and Printing, and Architectural Technology at Glasgow Caledonian University. He has worked for twenty years in interior design and architectural technology, and now specialises in computer animation for architecture.

In August 2013, John embarked on a long-held ambition: learning to draw. Equipped with some basic art materials and innumerable hours of online tutorials, he experimented with different styles and techniques and discovered a special talent for hyperrealism. John's reputation as an artist and illustrator continues to grow, with his prints selling internationally and locally through the Made in Stirling shop.

He recently released his début illustrated children's book, *Alphabet Zoo*, which was inspired by storytimes with his son, Joel.

Toolbox

Books:
Zen in the Art of Writing, Ray Bradbury
The Artist's Way, Julia Cameron
On Becoming a Novelist, John Gardner
Writing down the Bones, Natalie Goldberg
On Writing, Stephen King
Essentials of Spontaneous Prose, Jack Kerouac

Websites:
www.figmentpublishing.co.uk
www.lauraswriting.online
https://helenmackinven.wordpress.com
https://www.facebook.com/jmcpencilart

Miscellaneous:
Writer's Toolbox
Storycubes (Smart Phone App)
Figment Prompt Bot @6minute_prompts